JOSH ALLEN

THE BOY WHO BECAME A STAR QUARTERBACK

This book belongs to

_____

CONTENTS

CHAPTER 1

Small-Town Beginnings

Once upon a time, in a small town nestled among vast fields of golden wheat and swaying cornstalks, there lived a young boy named Josh Allen. Firebaugh, California, was not a place known for its bustling city life or towering skyscrapers. Instead, it was a place where the sun kissed the earth each morning, where neighbors waved to each other from across the street, and where community meant everything.

In this town, young Josh Allen spent his days exploring the wonders of nature. From chasing butterflies in the backyard to climbing trees with his friends, Josh was always on the lookout for adventure. But amidst his playful escapades, there was one thing that captured Josh's heart like nothing else: football.

Every evening, as the sun dipped below the horizon, Josh could be found in the backyard, tossing around a worn-out football with his dad, Joel. Joel, a hardworking man with calloused hands from long days in the fields, saw something special in his son's eyes. He knew that Josh had a gift—a gift for football.

As Josh grew older, his love for the game only deepened. He watched football games on TV with wide-eyed wonder, studying the moves of his favorite players and dreaming of the day when he would grace the same field as his heroes. But Firebaugh was not a town known for producing football stars. It was a town where dreams often faded beneath the weight of reality.

Yet, Josh refused to let the limitations of his surroundings define him. With each passing day, his determination burned brighter, fueled by the unwavering support of his family. His mother, LaVonne, a kind-hearted woman with a smile that could light up the darkest of nights, cheered him on from the sidelines, while his siblings, Jason and Mackenzie, stood by his side through thick and thin.

Josh's high school years were not just filled with athletic pursuits. Alongside his passion for sports, he balanced responsibilities on the family farm and contributed to his mother's restaurant in Firebaugh.

In the eyes of many recruiters, Josh may have been overlooked due to his physical stature and the fact that he didn't attend elite quarterback camps.

Despite the challenges that lay ahead, Josh Allen dared to dream big. With a football in hand and a heart full of hope, his journey from the fields of Firebaugh to the bright lights of the NFL was just beginning.

CHAPTER 2

College Years

Josh's journey continued as he headed off to Reedley College, a special place where he could pursue his love for football. During his time at Reedley College, Josh's talent shone bright. He led the team's offense with remarkable skill, helping them achieve some incredible rankings among all the junior colleges in California.

Despite facing some challenges at the beginning of the season, Josh never gave up. In one unforgettable game, he ran for four touchdowns after coming off the bench, proving that he was a true team player. Soon after, he became the team's starting quarterback, guiding them to victory with his powerful throws and quick thinking on the field.

But even though Josh's talent was clear to see, getting noticed by big colleges wasn't easy. Despite his coaches at Reedley thinking he'd receive many offers, Josh found himself facing disappointment. He sent emails to lots of college coaches, hoping for a chance to shine on a bigger stage, but only a few schools showed interest.

One of those schools was Wyoming, where Coach Bohl saw something special in Josh. He believed that Josh could be the face of their football program, and he even visited Josh's family farm to say so! Josh made the brave decision to commit to Wyoming, ready to start a new chapter in his football journey.

At Wyoming, Josh faced an injury that ended his first season early. With determination and hard work, Josh returned to the field stronger than ever, leading his team with passion and skill. In 2016, he threw for over 3,200 yards and 28 touchdowns.

As Josh's college career unfolded, he faced big decisions about his future. Should he declare for the 2017 NFL draft or stay in college for another year? With advice from his coaches, family, and even NFL star Carson Wentz, Josh ultimately chose to stay at Wyoming for another season, determined to continue chasing his dreams on and off the field.

CHAPTER 3

Draft Day and Rookie Season

In the world of football, there's a day that shines brighter than any other—the NFL Draft. For Josh Allen, this day wasn't just about football; it was about dreams taking flight and the promise of a new beginning. As the days leading up to the draft dwindled, Josh felt a mix of nerves and anticipation coursing through him. Every phone call, every interview, felt like a step closer to his destiny.

On draft day, the air crackled with excitement as Josh awaited his fate. Surrounded by family and friends, he watched the clock tick down, each second feeling like an eternity. But amidst the nerves, there was a spark of hope—a belief that today, everything could change.

Then, in a moment that felt like magic, the Buffalo Bills chose Josh as the seventh overall pick of the 2018 NFL Draft. Tears of happiness filled his eyes as he realized that his childhood dream was finally coming true. All those years of hard work, sacrifices, and unwavering dedication had led him to this incredible moment.

In 2018, Josh Allen donned the Buffalo Bills' jersey for his first NFL season. With each step onto the field, he carried the dreams of fans and the hopes of a team on his shoulders. Alongside his teammates, he trained hard during the offseason, eager to prove himself worthy of the starting quarterback position.

As the season opener approached, Josh faced tough competition from experienced quarterbacks A. J. McCarron and Nathan Peterman. Despite his impressive preseason performance, Josh began the season as Peterman's backup after McCarron was traded.

However, fate had other plans. On September 9, 2018, Josh Allen stepped onto the field for his very first regular season game against the Baltimore Ravens. He was given this chance after his teammate, Peterman, struggled during the match. Josh seized the opportunity to showcase his skills with 74 passing yards and 26 rushing yards.

On September 12, the Bills decided that Josh would be their starting quarterback for the upcoming game against the Los Angeles Chargers. In that game, Josh threw for 245 yards and scored his very first NFL passing touchdown to Kelvin Benjamin. Week after week, Josh faced both challenges and victories, with each moment contributing to his rising fame.

In Week 14, Josh faced off against fellow rookie Sam Darnold and the New York Jets. Josh scored a rushing touchdown and gained an impressive 101 yards on the ground. He made history by becoming the first quarterback ever to rush for at least 95 yards in three consecutive weeks, totaling 335 yards in that span.

But it was in Week 17 that Josh truly left his mark. Against the Miami Dolphins, he delivered a spectacular performance, scoring five total touchdowns and earning recognition as the AFC's Offensive Player of the Week.

As the season drew to a close, the Bills celebrated Josh's accomplishments, including being the first quarterback in team history to lead in both passing and rushing. Despite the ups and downs, Josh's rookie season was a testament to his grit, determination, and unwavering belief in himself.

CHAPTER 4

Rise to Stardom

As the 2019 season began, Josh Allen proudly became the starting quarterback for the Buffalo Bills, leading his team onto the field as their captain.

In Week 1, Josh displayed his resilience by leading the Bills to a thrilling comeback victory over the Jets. Despite facing a daunting 16-point deficit in the third quarter, Josh rallied his team to score 17 unanswered points. He achieved personal bests with 254 passing yards and 24 completions, securing a passing touchdown and a rushing touchdown, although he also faced two interceptions.

Throughout the season, Josh faced both triumphs and setbacks. In Week 3, he struggled against the Patriots' formidable defense but still managed to score an offensive touchdown, making him the first player to do so against the Patriots in the 2019 season.

A brief setback occurred when Josh suffered a helmet-to-helmet hit in a game against the Patriots, forcing him out of play due to concussion protocol. However, he returned the following week to lead the Bills to victory against the Titans, demonstrating his determination.

In Week 10, despite a valiant effort against the Browns, the Bills fell short due to missed field goal attempts. However, Josh bounced back in Week 11, delivering a stellar performance against the Dolphins, passing for three touchdowns and rushing for another, earning recognition as AFC Offensive Player of the Week.

As the season progressed, Josh continued to shine, delivering impressive performances against formidable opponents such as the Cowboys and the Steelers, securing crucial wins for the Bills.

Although the Bills narrowly missed out on the division title in a rematch against the Patriots, Josh's contributions throughout the season were undeniable. He finished the regular season with impressive statistics, including over 3,000 passing yards, 20 passing touchdowns, and nine rushing touchdowns.

Despite a heartbreaking loss in the AFC Wild Card Round against the Texans, Josh's efforts did not go unnoticed. He showcased his versatility by breaking franchise records and demonstrating his prowess as a quarterback, leaving fans eager to see what the future held for this promising young player.

In the 2020 season, Josh Allen's journey with the Buffalo Bills was remarkable, filled with triumphs, challenges, and moments that would go down in history.

Josh started the season with gusto, throwing for over 300 yards in three games in a row! He led the Buffalo Bills to exciting victories against the Jets, Dolphins, and Los Angeles Rams. In one game against Miami, he threw an incredible 415 yards, and in another game against Los Angeles, he helped the team make a thrilling comeback to win at the last minute.

Week after week, Josh's performances captivated fans and critics alike. From stunning comebacks to record-breaking feats, he left an indelible mark on the game of football. With his powerful throws, nimble footwork, and unwavering determination, Josh led the Bills to victories that would be remembered for years to come.

In the midst of his stellar season, Josh faced personal challenges as well. Tragically, he lost his grandmother, but even in the face of adversity, he showed remarkable strength and resilience, honoring her memory with every play.

Throughout the season, Josh continued to break franchise records and receive accolades along the way. He earned the title of AFC Offensive Player of the Week four times this season! Additionally, Allen and four of his teammates were honored with selections to the 2021 Pro Bowl. Josh also achieved second place in the MVP voting with four votes.

His leadership, skill, and determination propelled the Bills to new heights, culminating in their first AFC East division title in over two decades. With each game, Josh proved himself to be not just a star athlete, but a leader both on and off the field. His journey was a testament to the power of perseverance, passion, and dedication, inspiring fans everywhere.

In 2021, Josh Allen's journey continued with new milestones and exciting moments. It all began in May, when the Bills showed their confidence in him by extending his contract through the 2028 season. Then, during a thrilling game against the Dolphins in Week 2, Josh reached over 10,000 career passing yards!

Week 3 brought another triumph as Josh led the Bills to a fantastic victory against the Washington Football Team, passing for an incredible 358 yards and scoring five touchdowns! With this remarkable performance, he joined an elite group of players in NFL history.

But the excitement didn't stop there! In Week 5, Josh faced off against the Chiefs in a highly anticipated rematch. Despite facing tough competition, he showed his skill, throwing for 315 yards and three touchdowns, and rushing for another touchdown. The Bills emerged victorious with a 38-20 win, with Josh making history by achieving an outstanding 21 yards per completion.

Week after week, Josh continued to amaze fans with his talent and leadership on the field. Although there were ups and downs, including a tough loss to the Titans, Josh's resilience and determination never wavered.

As the season progressed, Josh's accomplishments piled up. In a thrilling game against the Buccaneers in Week 14, he led a remarkable comeback, rallying the team to 24 second-half points and surpassing 4,000 passing yards for the season.

Josh's dedication and hard work paid off. He finished the regular season with an impressive 4,407 passing yards, 36 passing touchdowns, and 763 rushing yards, earning him recognition as one of the league's top players.

In the Divisional Round, the Bills faced off against the Chiefs in a thrilling rematch. Allen threw two crucial touchdowns in the final two minutes of the game. Despite their best efforts, the Bills fell short in overtime, with the Chiefs winning 42–36.

Allen's performance was remarkable, matching Chiefs quarterback Patrick Mahomes throw for throw. He completed 27 of 37 passes for 329 yards and four touchdowns, and rushed for 68 yards. Allen's postseason performance earned him a record-breaking passer rating of 149.0, the highest ever in a single postseason, surpassing the legendary Joe Montana's previous record.

CHAPTER 5

Continued AFC East Success

In the 2022 season, Josh Allen delivered strong performances. One of the memorable moments came in a rematch against the Chiefs, reminiscent of their previous postseason encounter. Allen displayed his prowess with 329 passing yards and three touchdowns, leading the Bills to a come-from-behind 24–20 victory.

Allen continued to excel throughout the season, including a remarkable fourth-quarter comeback against the Jets and a Thanksgiving Day win against the Lions. With consistent performances, Allen helped the Bills clinch their third consecutive AFC East division title and secured a spot in the 2023 Pro Bowl Games as an initial roster selection for the AFC team.

In the 2023 season, Josh made history by becoming the first quarterback in NFL history to score 40 total touchdowns in four consecutive seasons. He also tied the NFL record for rushing touchdowns in a season by a quarterback, demonstrating his incredible talent throughout the season.

In the playoffs, Josh Allen and the Bills faced the Steelers in the Wild Card Round. Allen completed 21-of-30 passes for 203 yards and three passing touchdowns, helping the Bills secure a 31–17 victory. He also amazed everyone with a career-long 52-yard touchdown run, which became the longest rushing score in Bills' postseason history and the second-longest by a quarterback in NFL postseason history.

In the Divisional Round against the Chiefs at home, Allen played exceptionally well, contributing to all three of the Bills' touchdowns and gaining 258 of the team's total 368 yards. Despite his efforts, the Bills lost 27–24, ending their playoff journey in the Divisional Round for the third consecutive year.

CHAPTER 6

Beyond Football

Josh Allen isn't just a football player—he's also a philanthropist, someone who works to make the world a better place. One of the ways he does this is by supporting the John R. Oishei Children's Hospital in Buffalo.

As a spokesperson for the hospital, Josh does more than just talk about it. He visits the hospital, spends time with the patients, and even appears in commercials to help raise money. During the 2019 season, Josh donated $200 to the hospital for every touchdown he scored. That's a lot of money, and it goes to help kids who are sick get better.

After Josh Allen played a game following the death of his grandmother, Bills fans wanted to do something special to honor her memory. They donated money to the hospital in $17 increments, because that's Josh's jersey number. And guess what? By the end of the year, they had raised over $1 million!

In honor of all the donations, the hospital decided to name a new wing after Josh's grandmother, calling it the "Patricia Allen Pediatric Recovery Wing." Josh and his family were so touched by this gesture that they decided to start the "Patricia Allen Fund" to help even more kids in need.

But that's not all Josh does. He also supports other organizations, like the Leukemia & Lymphoma Society and the Jessie Rees Foundation, which help kids with cancer. And during the COVID-19 pandemic, Josh donated money to help people who were sick and needed medical care.

Josh Allen isn't just a hero on the football field—he's a hero in the community, too. And he shows us that no matter how big or small, we can all make a difference in the lives of others.

CHAPTER 7

Josh Allen's Inspiration

As we come to the end of Josh Allen's incredible journey, it's time to reflect on the legacy he leaves behind. From his humble beginnings to his rise as one of the NFL's brightest stars, Allen's story is one of perseverance, dedication, and unwavering determination.

Throughout his career, Allen has not only excelled on the football field but has also become a beacon of hope and inspiration for countless fans around the world. His passion for the game, combined with his tireless work ethic, has shown us all what it means to pursue our dreams with courage and conviction.

Allen's legacy extends far beyond his accomplishments on the gridiron. Through his charitable efforts and community outreach, he has made a lasting impact on the lives of others, proving that true greatness lies in lifting others up and making a difference in the world.

So as you turn the final pages of this book, let Josh Allen's story inspire you to pursue your own dreams with all your heart and to always strive for greatness. For in the end, it's not about the touchdowns scored or the records broken —it's about the legacy we leave behind and the lives we touch along the way. And in that regard, Josh Allen will forever be remembered as a hero.

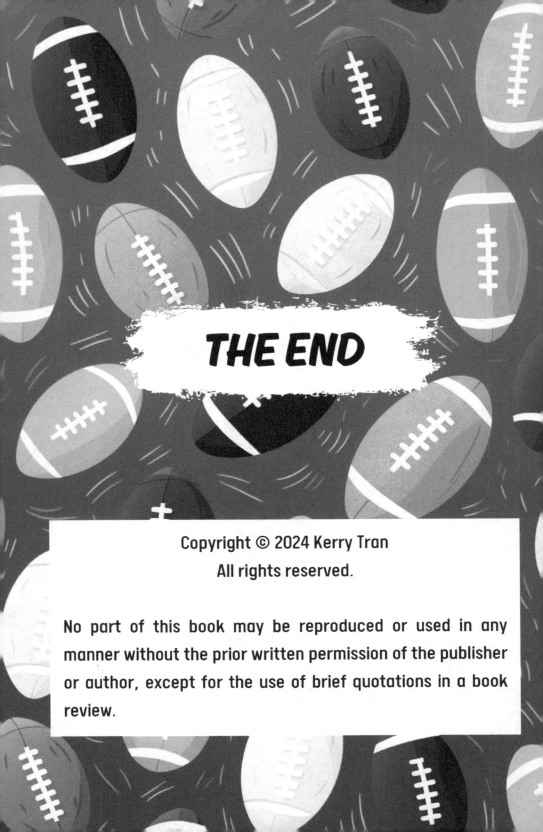

THE END